I0756239

FINISHING LINE PRESS
www.finishinglinepress.com

Morning of the World

poems by

Jane M. Wiseman

Finishing Line Press
Georgetown, Kentucky

Morning of the World

ISBN 979-8-89990-386-1 First Edition

ACKNOWLEDGMENTS

Morning of the World" was first published in *The Main Street Rag*
"Blue" was first published in *The Headlight Review*
"You, Who Are Gone" was first published in *NonBinary Review* #35, Old Friends issue
"Transatlantic Crossing" was first published in *The Ekphrastic Review*
"Descent Into the Cave" was first published in *The Westchester Review*
"A Visitation" was published in a slightly different form in *Euphony Journal*
"Yet You" was first published in *Sunspot Literary Journal*

Warm thanks to Jude Nutter and Amy Beeder for their great advice, and to the Poet Fools critique group of North Carolina and the poets of Madeline Island.

Publisher: Leah Huete de Maines
Editor: Christen Kincaid
Cover Art: Photo-manipulated detail from the author's painting
Morning Light, Sandia Mountains, Albuquerque, New Mexico
Author Photo: Jonathan Conklin
Cover Design: Elizabeth Maines McCleavy

Order online: www.finishinglinepress.com
also available on amazon.com

Author inquiries and mail orders:
Finishing Line Press
PO Box 1626
Georgetown, Kentucky 40324
USA

Contents

Morning of the World

If not for the bare feet of the sanctified,
the tight-coiled river would not have bent
to the depths of the delta, cup of the heartdeep
rinsed out, never poured, and

none of us would have gone trooping
over the high hill where the sun called
each blade of bluestem glittering
beneath its burden of dew, where the quail
sprang from their thickets as we forged
a green path to the shifting bars of sands.

Dream-splintered, capsuled, none
would have come there, none of us
come to be known. We would have stayed small
if not for that.

as. . . as

as the cosmic fume
bubbles up universes
from out of the lattice
arranging reality

as, arrowing
the halcyon waves,
kingfisher presses tight
between sky and sea

as Jupiter risen a jewel
over the lake
hangs in velvet night
with his red eye

as the oak outside my window
whispers secrets
to summer, then sheds
its acorns entire

as the infant draws breath,
as the child waxes prime,
as the shriveling inward, so I

You, Who Are Gone

Lacework of lives twists together. Then
the pattern warps down other paths.
I, too young and stupid to notice. You,
too young and stupid to make me see.

Briefly we threaded again together, I,
in trouble with life, you with something
meaningful you made. Though silk extruded
from the spinneret is strong, it can't hold forever.
And so our lives sheared apart. Again. Again.

I'd like to say I felt a strand give when you went,
as if, feeling along the weft, I could sense the way
the trembling shivers the whole line.

Stalking the woods, some careless force—
hunter, animal—comes upon a dew-pearled web
so glistening the sun stands still in awe of it.

Something blunders to the center. The marvelous
tatters in shreds and residue across the selvage
of the field into the dark places beneath pines.

Why did I not feel to my bones the void
you made in sunlight's fabric? Why could I not
reknit the world's unraveling?

The wind's word

teaches us to speak it. The wind's name
hushes and swerves the wild field, bending over
the grasses. Above the three of us, the gust of it
rushes clouds across, we, sleeved between.
Me. Shaun. The other one, I can't remember his name,
only the green of his eyes.

Twilight deepens and rises. A star pokes a hole
at the zenith, then another so the gold shines through.
And one of us looks out new people, new things,
new kinds. One of us hangs back, caught up
on a hook of sky. And one of us dies young before
he happens far. His name soughs in the land's breath,
trembles, twigs tapping, clacking together,
clash and moan and jar.

A dream tangled in the net of the eye

gossamer, released, it will fly,
it will dart from window to tree
to the boglands beyond the hold,
soar free until it comes apart,
motes of desire tossed in the air
from sill to oak to swale.
You may open the sash. Will
some of its essence be there still,
will it come to your call,
fragments long dispersed
leaving only feathery residue
to rub between finger and thumb?
By then it will be a gone thing
far down the road past
the house of memory or your recall.
No more does it know your name
if, a wild thing, ever it did. By now
I doubt it knows its own. By
nightfall, become other.
By midnight wholly belong
or maybe only partly, seed
rooting, crystal on its lattice
growing, to another.

Like a candle

Before she died, my mother blazed
like a candle in its revealing,
a waxen core. Before she died,
guttered out like a candle,
the flame of her leaning back
the way a flame will,
in the opening of a door. Before
she died my mother stood up
tall as a candle, wick freshly
trimmed, and she leaned back
buffeted, the wind of the opening
of a door. Before she died, she
dwindled, a candle burning
to last liquid murmurs of wax.
Flamed up, wick charcoaled,
broken, fell inward into
wax. Stub of an ember only
left glowing. The tip of it,
glowing. Whisper of smoke,
rising, a column reaching,
sigh and waft and wind.

My father the child, deep in the garden.

Here's the vista, here's the golden hedge,
studded yellow flowers popped forth
overnight, and there below, the fringe
of reeds circling and invading the froth
of the languished pond. Gate and hinge
to the spell-struck seat strewn with the duff,
the needles of tall firs, enchanted ledge
enclosed, romance of the opened book
turned to an open page. A place to hoard
childhood's seeming liquid sunlit glance,
last royal dreaming, last throne.
Soon, the scion, he steps to the board,
proper game-piece in its square and stance.
Gallant knight? King, even? Here, the pawn.

Shoreline

Stones are like a man,
but a woman's born
oceanic.

A man stands mute on the shore
under sun and rain,
stringent as weather.
Just as sad.

A woman grows gills, sways
with the tide rolling in,
yearns as it rolls back out.
She coalesces into salty pools.
Her briny hair is green. Suckers
roughen her undersides. She rimples down
when seas get tall. Squadrons
of pelicans, wave-topping, plunge
with her to depth. She offers
to them a fish, a crab, a shell.

At times the sediment
of a man,
if sifted through,
carefully worked in situ
with small picks and delicate brushes,
reveals,
pressed between layers
of calcified mud,
the imprint
of her frond.

Blue

Was it April? I'd moved into that drab place
up Maple and you—remember this?—
came over with wine, with oysters, even,
snagged from the fish market past the canal.
Can you see it? I can:

We've spread our feast on the bare boards,
not a stick of furniture in there, no table
for any of it. Spring fingers of sunlight
go probing, lengthening, stippling
until all the tall windows blank out blue.

Remember how our bodies reached
and touched and tasted, arms, hands,
lips, how our limbs entangled
on the hardwood stretch of floor, how
our murmurs, then cries gave us back
their muted echoes from the high dusty
moldings of the ceiling, and drifted down.

How the moments became one moment,
how they made one place where we
stepped out of time.

                    Too much later, how
blue time rushed us and mauled us,
holding us in its cruel jaw. Drove into us
the cruel blue of its tooth.

Transatlantic Crossing

Marsden Hartley paints John Donne in his shroud

If an ocean-going liner traveling at let's say
twenty-three knots not fast enough quite to win
the Blue Riband crosses the path of the

They stood out from the bay at five o'clock
in the light of dawn entered by eight close after
he witnessed from the deck some galleon
commanded by Devereaux or maybe de Vere

Let's say Nicholas Stone worked from a
drawing of Donne in his shroud then awkward
Martin Droeshout tried an engraving it's just fact
the statue itself survived the Great Fire stands
now at St. Paul's

Let's say this shy young man gay diffident retiring
beneath Mount Katahdin The Painter of Maine dies
quietly alone before he does let's say traveling a
contemplative 2mph but halting at shore at mountain to
observe let's say crosses the path of the man

Who knowing death approaches takes to his
shroud and won't get out of it let's say a man
marked by the perishing away of Henry his brother
dead in Newgate for his faith let's say a man who abjured
that faith and took another let's say a man who loved
one woman his whole life fought for his king let's say
a man convinced of his sin but forced anyway into
holy orders becomes the most celebrated preacher of his

Let's say these two cross paths over
the Atlantic over the centuries let's say
they do let's say no calculation parses the place
where the two of them burst each one from his point
Euclidean primitive notion to the intersection that holds up
the world. Let's say if they did not the world would collapse on itself.
Let's say it would.

It's Just About the Weather pantoum

Rain masses over the fields, hisses incessantly down.
Green lands undress to gray. The houses drown.
Where are you going, my sister, my brother, my love?
To the market to spend and sell and make my trove.

The lands scour in a sea of gray. The houses drown.
All that was green molders and snarls to brown.
Those in the market strive to fadge their trove,
selling and spending and gaining, scrape and save.

All that is green grudges and turns brown.
Gullies wash out. Birds refuse their song, trees their gown.
Scurry to sell and shove and scrape and save!
Every woman's a cheat, every man's a knave.

Too long, too late the land lies under its swoon.
Where are you going, my brother, my sister, my love?
Nothing here to gain, nothing to scrape, to save.
Rain slants over spent fields, hisses incessantly down.

Descent Into the Cave

At some point, we must uncouple.
The overhang, you see, is a maw.
Before you go, inscribe your name
on the tablet of members. Incise it
with your own chisel, tap it in with your own
hammer, refine it with your own rasps and
rifflers. Time. Please adjust your harness.
Light your lamp. It will help with the
early stages. Later, only an impediment.
Discard it then. You'll know when. Ready?
We'll escort you, one of us vigilant
on either side, to the ramp, to the
ever-narrowing crevices. Abrasions,
a natural part of the process, and
the odd amputation. Drop into the egg
of the place. Crouch over, nose to knees.
Make no sound. You've arrived.

Dream-ghosts

Down to the deeps again where something
grabs, something forces itself, sometimes
smothering, sometimes snipping the tether
and letting me soar. Which will it be this night,
hag or winged one?

Slip through the portal, kneel in the vestibule,
wait the disgorgement of invaders.
The mort-safe may keep me in, but it does not
keep them out. No string in the dark
to clutch, ring the above-ground bell,
alert the waked ones, hope they dig me free.

I lie straightened into my narrow bed,
pounding on the low ceiling as these
night walkers sift through every orifice.
At the narthex of my ear they corkscrew
whispered hermeneutics through the corridors
of the domed cathedral brain.

When you wake (they tell me),
you will not remember this, or if you do,
you'll think we babbled nonsense.

But we have told you:

> Who you are, you
> who lie in thrall to dreaming.
>
> What ribs and buttresses you've hoisted
> to shore up, in vain, your void.
>
> What deeds you swear you'll undertake
> in penance for your occupation of this earth.

May I not warn others?

Let them seek their own messengers
swarming out of their own
merciless dark.

Taking Ship

I, this pronoun, nosing into
that stone passageway,
the sentence. What
verbs it? Where do I ride?

Etched deep, the red strait
through which thought
comes birthing. Who knows how
it tosses out its parcel of words,

cargo bursting its carton and spilling.
The sentence: channel, tunnel.
The sentence a winnowing,
shucking off all other possible

garments, buttoning
into this coat only. Heavy weather.
On every setting-forth, there
in the offing hangs the harr.

Everything Only Always a Story

She disposes herself at the casement,
her tresses, her baubles, her gown.

Below in the garden he waits,
easy beneath the smooth cool skin
of a rock. His bulbs of eyes, glowing.
The blunt seemly cut of his snout.
Holstered, the long sticky tongue,
yet poised at a sign to roll out.
The sun's liquid finger finds him,
to stipple the spots of his back,
the rivers of stripes tapering
to the nub where in careless youth
he sported a tail. Admire the rapid dap-dap
of his elegant throat where it pulses.
Admire how green.

She, looking down from the window,
does not dream he's there. If she should
catch him and case him in a copper pot
with holes for the ants to come in,
she could boil his picked-clean carcass down.
Out of one side, she might pluck the bone
that silences, that stills the boiling of water.
Out of the other, the bone that assuages
the fury of dogs, Apocynon; assuages the quartan.
Cools the overheat, frivol of glances, kisses
behind fans, riotous blood.

                                        Or she could
keep him close in a box. The natterjack.
The brambletoad. Feed him and milk him
of all essences. Oh, then she'd sing.

The one pure jewel, bezoar, toadstone
of power, shines reliquary at the center
of his head. He squats in the filigreed casing
of her garden, underlaid fecund and steaming,
velvet with rot, bursting with bloom.

Big Straw Tourist Sombrero

1.
God only knows
where she got it.
My grandmother
never set foot
in Mexico.

2.
It comes to me now:
on the way to the beach.
Some tacky weedy place
down the back roads
of South Carolina
just this side of the
Gaffney Peach.

3.
A Walt Disney
kind of a hat from the
South Atlantic Coast
as remote from Old Mejico
as Alpha Centauri.
As far away as
childhood, soles of the feet
burning against tar,
then sand,
my grandfather's
pot belly, his sparse white
chest hairs, and her face,
my grandmother's,
as she sidles in
for her modest dip.

4.
Summer after summer
we rotted beneath
that hat. It grew dustier,

more tatty affixed
to the lattice of
that old woman's
big back porch,
and I dare to say darker
each year from the smoke
of her Luckies.
Summers in twilight.
Red-blood faux-exotic
straw circle. The ghost-white
criss-cross of lath.

5.
We kids darting, hiding
in the deep back yard
stretching all the way
to creosote tracks. Calling,
trapping hands down
on lightning bugs winking
their futile SOS. The grownups
underneath the hat
smoking and watching us,
talking sultry July,
disappointing Dow,
Korea.

6.
Far away
beneath the
dug chug grunt
of mill machinery,
a long whistle
floating,
nine o'clock train.

Wide Load

The city comes to a stop, all of us
halted and peering. The cops
with their shrieking whistles, all
the dumb faces peering up
through dirty windshields, all
idling dumbstruck except
one guy, red-faced beside me,
his mouth caved into a howl,
gesturing, leaning furious
on his horn as if that will help, but
past him over the dusty carapaces
of Chevys, Fords, Nissans towers
what? A majesty, a long sheen chained
to the long bed of a trailer of a truck,
bronze enormity. A petal? A machine?
We gape as it lofts us by, as the cops,
its acolytes, summon it, reverently
conjure it past the snarled traffic,
delicate immense bulk of it worming
articulate down the snaked vein of the city,
progressing into the stone forest of the city,
floating toward that beating clotted heart.

Superb Starling

Lamprotornis superbus, Ngorongoro crater

Fancy a place where the starlings flaunt themselves
this fancy, not the gray flock dropping blight
upon drab trees of the public park squared up
in sidewalks strewn with trash. Instead
a place where every bird cocks a jaunty crest,
feathers slashing scarlet in dim glades.

Fancy an Edenic bowl, caldera once volcanic
now exploded and extinct, such bounty
you know the first light of the world shone down
to conjure it and name it good.

Fancy drifting unburdened and unmoored
from the bright rim spiraling into lush depths,
soul detached from the unforgiving body,
full and fruitful of that green light, that green grace.

Fancy such a place.

The Ancestors

At the heart of every ring they made,
they forged the glyph for *weep*.
Along the wax-rubbed skin
of every cup they carved, the word
for *dread*, silvered in the wood.

Tell us their tales again, tell them over,
turn them and heft them as smooth stones
counted and towered. Stack them
year by year. At the base of each,
dig out a *why*, a *wonder*.

Take down the cracked photograph,
and smooth it. Try to make their figures out.
You can't do it. Time has wedged between.
Winds have spoken *cease*. The old seas
have seized and rinsed them,

foundered them in their pinnace,
cast them onto the shelving off,
scar unbridgeable. Mists scarve
to blind them, etch into the present
their old *no*, like acid.

A Glimpse

They gave me only a day.
They gave me only
a day of this. All the light,
all the green. The children
leaping in their flimsy dresses,
dragonflies wheeling, needles
darning the edge of the pond,
and I to move among them,
their music on my lips.
Only a day, only a day of this,
before I fade to background,
turn to climb again into dark places,
the tunnels, twists of my own estate,
pull down and lock the sashes,
pull shut my gates.

The Hinge

Threading along the escarpment to ease
down the ridge and around to the valley,
the trail switches through pillars,
maple stands and hemlock, carving splinters
of shadow from green lulls of air.
Birdsong washes the silence blue and gold,
redstarts migrating through, high
in the canopy, rocking and flitting,
holding the planet at poise.

They cease. Green rushes back to the gaps
between boles of trees. As if I peered up drowned
from the wavering bed of some stilled pool,
a fringe of trees glimpsed through green waters.
Drifting in slow current, lazy eddies of leaves
already crisped at the edges, a few turned red.
Time to surface, breathe true autumn.
The redstarts ready their pilgrimage.

Soon the season where all life thins,
black outlines of trees against drifts frozen
to short stiff peaks demarking furrows
of rumpled fields. The air's hum dampens,
redstarts flown. Listen. A great door
creaks open, leaking out of me
the green world. Letting winter in.

On the Sixth Day, Eve

Opened my eyes on light, a dazzle
through branches, opened my ears on the still
of new earth, my nostrils on its funk. God scooped up
a kaolin handful, spat on it, pinch-pot body, knob
of head. He soldered in the senses. Kneaded
the arms, legs, squat little torso. Reached me
down on the prickle of grass, set another
beside me. God pressed our hands together until
we joined. He diffused away between new trees,
your hand mashed hard into mine.

Finger by finger, I disengaged what God had done.
Out of the earth-mouth God had made,

I want to be that, not this.

                                                From a dry soul,
I panted for the stream, one of the four rivers
that ran past and over our feet, softening us and
dissolving.

          Or no, that.
                                          Eden's breeze came up. I waved
my earth-hand through the cool.

Ah. No. This. This.

I pointed through the overhang to where
the sun, a white fierce hole, hissed
from the young hot sky. I went out the gate,
walked into fire, into its eye,
into the wildness, out of the shade,
underneath that burning new-cast star.

Haboob at Lent

A wall of it, see how it bulges up
three thousand feet. Summer's
usually the time for it. Not
this transgressive season.
Planes collide. Wrong-way birds
wind up in Costa Rica. Semis
jackknife on I-40. Parallel,
on Old Route 66, Lolita shrieks,
grabs after her scarf, chiffon
ribboning the updraft off the blacktop
juddering behind them. Humbert laughs.
Waves unrolling, clouds of grains of it
scour across the land; bigger grains
saltate and ping-pong, dirty hailstorm
riding gap-winds blasting the flanks
of the Sandias. The drought-lands lift,
waver out to nowhere. They turn ash.
We all go blind. *Dust you are*, the wind
hoots and sheets, chasing us down.
To dust you shall return.

Cast Adrift at Dream's White Rock

for A.S.

Beneath pitted crags of lava buffered
in surf, hidden, irregular-blotched
black on white, small, slender,
poison, shy, the eel
within its silty bed

hard by the turtle beach.
These others lumber out
majestic, amniote
and ectotherm, sages
Permian, Triassic, Eocene.
Turtles surge the waves
onto the sand shelf, hunker
flippers up, eyes hooded,
ancient folds of skin. Carapace,
once read like wisdom. Plastron,
script of shell and bone, first
of all signs, first alphabet.

The eel gapes its mouth, feeds
on small fish schooling by.
Who knows what lies behind
occluded lenses of that eye.
Like Tiresias (or he or she like it),
starts out clothed one sex, then
puts on the other, oracle
of the patient cave.

In the visible universe,
it's turtles.
Turtles
all the way down.

Invisible, the worm,
tail in mouth, insinuates
eternity. And you, the lost,

submerged those endless fathoms, eyeless,
where you have no signs. You,
who have no words.

The U.S. Navy has outfitted them to detect explosives, but it takes seven or eight to get an accurate reading

About grasshoppers, yeah, remove their feet.
The spiny bits on the legs will stick in your throat.
Don't eat too many, especially those from fields of crops
whose farmers revile them, alongside thrips and aphids,
as pests. Smallholders and crofters have been known
to curse and spit. Grasshoppers have been known
to curse and spit. Forever chemicals may taint the wild ones.
Watch out for those. Buy them pre-packed, dehydrated,
settled down. They bring wisdom. They bring a little
extra protein. Some say they have a nutty flavor. Take care.
You could be allergic to chitin. Savory umami. Mushroomy,
earthy. A chewy, meaty texture. Feed them mint,
they'll taste minty. Try them on a cast-iron griddle
over a slow fire. Salt them. They date from the early Triassic.
Their jump is a three-stage process. Most of the day they spend

stridulating.

          I spend most of my day

                              stridulating.

They undergo incomplete metamorphosis, instar to instar,
each time larger. I undergo incomplete metamorphosis,
this I know. The ancient Greeks
employed them in atropropaic magic.

Use my husk as an amulet.

Go on, try it.

See if it helps.

At the Boundary

I am appropriating this container,
I am putting my stones and shards inside.

Forgive me, all you great practitioners of ghazal.
Half-sunk into a field of mud, this jar.

Wringing out laundry on the steps of your temple.
Scribbling the laundry list up your walls.

I know it's spring when all the grains fall hissing.
Time to turn the glass over, and I see the flaw.

Wicks die back to cinder, candles dwindling.
Snap down the shades. Shut the door.

The garden's overgrown this long gray season.
Webs of moss wind up the flanks of trees.

This gate swings on broken hinges. The path's only weeds.
No verse, just one drawn out ragged breath.

Who would have thought to end like this? No sound, no song.
Spatter of rain. After such a struggle, too. It's gone.

Up Whiteside Mountain

On certain days, as the stream choirs
through crevices of early spring,
when we're making pilgrimage to the overlook,
or winding up highway 64 at Bearpen Road
to trails carved into the forest
by the Cherokee, by the Muskogee, both
to go down in the crossfire of white greed for land;

days when we've tracked to its headwaters
the Chatooga River at Cashiers Lake
and the balm of the world lies on us
as benediction;

                                        on days like these we pause
at the cliffs' footings, weatherings of sills
of pluton into stark sheer drops, then make the climb
to the oldest peak in North America,
hurdling the Eastern Divide. Shading our eyes,
we peer across millennia as far as Africa,
gneiss from which this land wrenched
at the time of the rending of the earth.

They say Spearfinger roams
the tumbled rockfalls, her warnings unheeded,
but in this season the Shadow of the Bear
does not threaten over the folds of vales;
the wind there carries to us faintly
hooded warblers heady in their hymns.

We set our foot to a scoured space.
Pinxters' bells toll us counterpoint
through aisles of white pine and pitch pine.
Morels probe from under galax there,
and the fiddleheads unfurl their croziers,
consecrate for us the new-made sun.

A Visitation

In the blackout storm, our wings
shear through ravages of cloud
seen only in flashes. Compassing
our trackway toward you, we wheel
into dirty weather.

We bring you gifts: A feather.
A pebble. We bring you stems
of bracken. We bring a heart.

Above you, we murmur
among ourselves on the rooftree,
the puttering, the paltering
of our nails just audible
beneath thunder, the spouts and gusts
of rain rattling the sashes.

You thought you dreamed us.

When you wake, we come in sunlight,
sheen of morning on our backs.
Our beaks full of birrs and musicks, we bow
to lay our favor at your feet.

We have crossed your threshold.
We have claimed your shelter.

Yet You

anything they said was said slap on it
but what you said came out of the red deep

had a nostril big as a person could sit in it
feet like the sailing off the golden sheen

anything they did they did like one two three
but yours was a silver purse for fishes and fronds

you hauled it up the holy bronze of the deck
across the boards you spilled for only me

the dreams they dreamed were small and gray
dreams of yours towered to thunderheads

drifting the continent oh I could feel
the lightning flash from the dark underside
and the leading boil of it sang shrill and green

The way clause rides poem

as clauses tumble downhill
seeking the level of line

the way the line of the river will,
lazing through oxbow

the bow of the lower lip, how you might
draw it, curve of the loved cheek

curving impossibly down the neck
and into the body's rhyme.

*

Never stopping, shedding gravity,
moving beyond the Kármán line,

time's arrow will line out over the ecliptic,
orbit's plane, to tack

through clouds of comets, steer
past heliosphere.

In that place beyond, they neither marry
nor are they given in marriage

but oh the body, the part of you I loved, nor
arrow of it ever stopped.

*

The clauses that make the line,
the feathering of strokes of the pen,
do they come to the end, or
always point beyond?

Child in the back yard. With bubbles.

The shape of a life, long tail twisting
hollow gossamer as it bells off the mouth
of the wand, billows and wavers out walling
into the howl of the winds of the world,
turns, dwindles, merges to the gale

as she runs on

as she runs future to present

as she runs past

It’s a new day

Praise another one. The light streaming
in. Praise oblongs of light
from clerestory windows.
Praise the green.

Praise the scent of autumn
oncoming. Praise rain.

Praise the long vista down
4th avenue to the river.
Praise that.

Praise the vision
of the white buildings risen
along the braided river
tumbled across the land
and on down south.

Praise eyes and lips.
Praise hands. Throats.
Even the nosy neighbor
standing in the street
by the rows of mailboxes,
lonely,
without her teeth.

Praise the oiled roads
leading out of town
into the countryside,
and the gravel.

Canopies of maple.
Yammer of squirrel, sleepy call,
bird at midday,
some sparrow. Some wren.
Fields stretch dark beneath trees.
Praise them.
Praise these.

Jane Wiseman, a transplanted southeasterner from small-town Virginia, is a poet who now splits her time between the rural Sandia Mountains of New Mexico and very urban south Minneapolis. Living and working in so many different kinds of places has enriched her work.

Her chapbook *The Bee Telephone* won the 2024 Jonathan Holden chapbook competition. Her poems have appeared in such journals as *The Headlight Review, Southern Poetry Review, Main Street Rag*, and others.

Her undergraduate degree is from Duke University. She holds graduate degrees from the University of Illinois (Urbana) and the University of Pennsylvania.

www.ingramcontent.com/pod-product-compliance
Lightning Source LLC
LaVergne TN
LVHW090539110826
845146LV00003B/1187